Overview *Jeni's Lettuce*

Jeni and her dad plant lettuce, but the birds eat it.

Reading Vocabulary Words	**High-Frequency Words**	
worked	*hungry*	*today*
breakfast	*going*	*yes*
helping	*make*	*can*
	now	*good*

Building Future Vocabulary

* These vocabulary words do not appear in this text. They are provided to develop related oral vocabulary that first appears in future texts.

Words:	*morning*	*path*	*healthy*
Levels:	Green	Blue	Green

Comprehension Strategy
Recognizing cause and effect

Fluency Skill
Changing voice to differentiate speakers

Phonics Skill
Adding phonemes to change words (is – this, we – went, the – then, the – they)

Reading-Writing Connection
Copying a phrase

Home Connection
Send home one of the Flying Colors Take-Home books for children to share with their families.

Differentiated Instruction
Before reading the text, query children to discover their level of understanding of the comprehension strategy — Recognizing cause and effect. As you work together, provide additional support to children who show a beginning mastery of the strategy.

Focus on ELL
- Show children a picture of a garden and name items in it, helping children associate those items with the correct English terms.

- Explain that people grow both vegetables and flowers in gardens.

T1

Using This Teaching Version

1. Before Reading

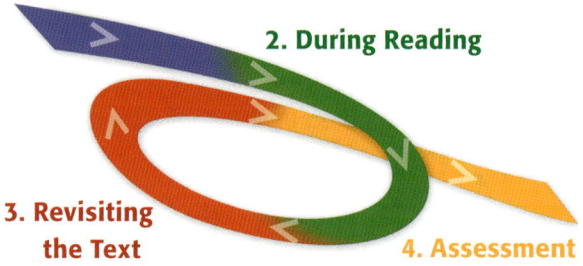

2. During Reading

3. Revisiting the Text

4. Assessment

This Teaching Version will assist you in directing children through the process of reading.

1. **Begin with Before Reading** to familiarize children with the book's content. Select the skills and strategies that meet the needs of your children.

2. **Next, go to During Reading** to help children become familiar with the text, and then to read individually on their own.

3. **Then, go back to Revisiting the Text** and select those specific activities that meet children's needs.

4. **Finally, finish with Assessment** to confirm children are ready to move forward to the next text.

1 Before Reading

Building Background

- Write the word *garden* on the board. Read it aloud and discuss with children what a garden is. Ask *What kind of plants grow in a garden?*

- Introduce the book by reading the title, talking about the cover illustration, and sharing the overview.

Building Future Vocabulary
Use Interactive Modeling Card: Word Wheel

- Introduce the word *healthy*. Discuss what people can do to stay healthy. Write children's responses on the top half of the Word Wheel.

- Have children suggest activities that are not healthy. Write them on the bottom half of the Word Wheel.

Introduction to Reading Vocabulary

- On blank cards write: *worked*, *breakfast*, and *helping*. Read them aloud. Tell children these words will appear in the text of *Jeni's Lettuce.*

- Use each word in a sentence for understanding.

Introduction to Comprehension Strategy

- Explain that the phrase *cause and effect* means that one action makes something else happen.
- Have children turn to the title page of *Jeni's Lettuce*. Discuss that when Jeni tips the watering can, water comes out.
- Tell children they will be looking for examples of cause and effect in *Jeni's Lettuce*.

Introduction to Phonics

- Write the word **this** on the board. Explain that by changing only one sound in the word, represented by a letter or letters, children can form new words. Erase the letters *th*. Have children say this new word: **is**.
- Write the word **we**, then change it to **went**. Have children say this new word.
- Write the word **can** on the board, and have children brainstorm other words that can be formed by changing the last letter. (**cat**, **cap**, **car**, **cab**)

Modeling Fluency

- Read aloud page 6, modeling different voices for Jeni and her father.
- Talk about changing voices to show that a different character is speaking. Explain that this helps listeners better understand what's going on.

2 During Reading

Book Talk

Beginning on page T4, use the During Reading notes on the left-hand side to engage children in a book talk. On page 16, follow with Individual Reading.

During Reading

Book Talk

- **Comprehension Strategy** Have children turn to the title page illustration. Ask *What is Jeni doing?* (watering her lettuce) *What happens to plants when you water them?* (It helps them grow.)

- Ask *What is the action taking place, or the cause?* (watering) *What is the result, or effect, of this action?* (Plants grow.)

- Explain that sometimes not taking an action also has an effect. Ask *What would be the effect of not watering the lettuce?* (It would die.)

Turn to page 2 – Book Talk

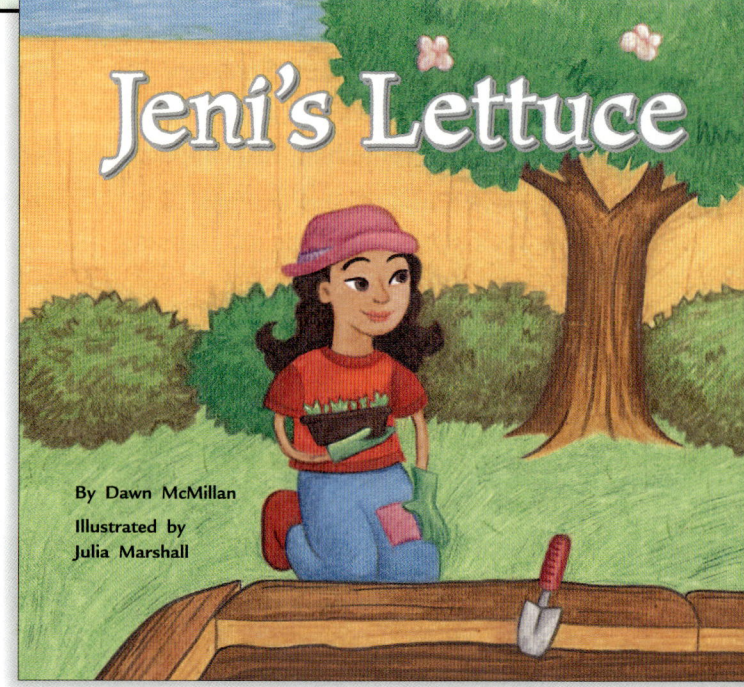

T4

Revisiting the Text

Future Vocabulary

- Look at the title page. Ask *Is there a clue that tells us the lettuce is healthy?* (Yes, the lettuce is green.) *What is Jeni doing to keep the lettuce healthy?* (watering it)

Now revisit pages 2–3

During Reading

Book Talk

- Ask *What meal is Dad making?* (breakfast) *What are Jeni and Dad going to eat for breakfast?* (toast, coffee, milk, something in a pot) *Is Jeni helping Dad?* (No, she is watching him.)

- **Comprehension Strategy** Say *Find Dad's cup of coffee on the breakfast table. Is the coffee hot or cold?* (hot) *This is the result, or effect, of some action. What action might have made the coffee hot?* (Dad heated it in the coffeepot or on the stove.)

- Ask children to look at the illustration. Say *Jeni's glass contains milk. What action made this happen?* (pouring milk from the carton into the glass)

Turn to page 4 – Book Talk

"Dad! It is Saturday today!" said Jeni.
"Today we are going to make the new garden. Can we do it now?"

"I'm hungry," said Dad.
"We will eat breakfast. Then we will make the garden."

Revisiting the Text

Future Vocabulary

- Ask *Does this story start in the morning, afternoon, or evening?* (morning) *What clues tell you that the story starts in the morning?* (Jeni and Dad are wearing pajamas and making breakfast.) *What do you like to eat in the morning?* (cereal, toast, eggs)

Now revisit pages 4–5

During Reading

Book Talk

- Ask *What are Jeni and Dad doing?* (work*ing in the garden*) *Are they* work*ing hard?* (yes) *What are they planting?* (lettuce) *How can you tell?* (from the title of the book)

- Have children locate the words *breakfast* and *worked* on these pages. Ask *What does it mean that Jeni and Dad* worked*?* (They did a job or chore.)

- **Comprehension Strategy** Have children look at the illustration. Point out that the soil in the garden is lumpy on the left side and smooth on the right side. Ask *Why is the soil on the right side smooth?* (Jeni is raking the soil.) Say *The action is raking. The result is smooth soil. The raking causes the smooth soil.*

Turn to page 6 — Book Talk

Jeni and Dad had breakfast. Then they went to the garden. They worked and **worked** in the new garden.

4

"This is a good garden," said Jeni.

"Yes," said Dad.
"Here is the lettuce.
It can go here."

Revisiting the Text

Future Vocabulary
- Say *Dad and Jeni are working. Does working keep people healthy?* (yes) *What are some jobs around your home that would keep your body strong and healthy?* (sweeping the floor, taking out garbage, planting and weeding a garden, raking leaves)

- **Comprehension Strategy** Point out that working is an action, or cause, that has a result, or effect. Ask children to name some effects of working. (staying healthy, getting a job done, earning money)

Now revisit pages 6–7

During Reading

Book Talk

- Have children find the word *helping*. Ask *Is Jeni helping Dad?* (yes) *How will Jeni help Dad?* (by planting lettuce)
- **Phonics Skill** Have children find the word *in* on page 6. Ask *What words can you form by replacing* n *with another letter? (it, is)*

Turn to page 8 – Book Talk

"I will help you
with the lettuce, Dad," said Jeni.

"Good!" said Dad.
"I like you helping me
in the garden."

Revisiting the Text

Future Vocabulary
- Ask children to look at page 7. Ask *Do Jeni and Dad look healthy?* (yes) *What do Jeni and Dad do to stay healthy?* (work in the garden, eat healthy foods) Encourage children to list healthy and unhealthy activities. Ask *Does eating lettuce help Jeni and Dad stay healthy?* (yes)

Now revisit pages 8–9

During Reading

Book Talk

- Ask *After planting the garden, did Jeni and Dad eat breakfast?* (no, lunch) *Do we know if Jeni helped Dad make lunch?* (no)
- Ask *What has happened to the lettuce Jeni and Dad planted?* (Most of it has disappeared.)
- **Comprehension Strategy** Say *Look at page 9. How would you describe the look on the faces of Jeni and Dad?* (surprised or confused) *What is causing this look?* (Most of the lettuce is missing.)

Turn to page 10 — Book Talk

Jeni and Dad had lunch. Then they went back to the garden.

Jeni looked for the lettuce.

Revisiting the Text

Future Vocabulary

- Ask children to look at page 8. Ask *What are Jeni and Dad walking on as they leave the house?* (a path) *What are paths for?* (walking on, showing the right direction, protecting grass) *What can paths be made from?* (rock, soil, concrete, sand)

- Discuss the word *path* with children. Ask children why paths are useful and important. (make walking easier, show you where to go)

- Explain that a path can be more than something people walk on. Say *A path can be an idea that shows us what to do in life. What do we mean when we follow the path to good health?* (We do what is needed to be healthy.)

Now revisit pages 10–11

9

During Reading

Book Talk

- Say *I see many plants in the garden. There are trees, bushes, and grass.* Ask *Why do you think the birds only ate the lettuce?* (They like lettuce better than the other plants.) *Are the birds helping Jeni and Dad?* (no)

- **Fluency Skill** Have children read page 10 in Dad's voice. Ask *How would Dad sound if he was angry? How would he sound if he was sad?*

- **Comprehension Strategy** Remind children that an action causes a result. Say *The result on these pages is that the lettuce is gone. What action caused this result?* (The birds ate the lettuce.)

Turn to page 12 — Book Talk

Revisiting the Text

Future Vocabulary
- Ask *Is it still morning? How do you know?* (No, we know it is afternoon because Jeni and Dad have eaten lunch.)

Now revisit pages 12–13

During Reading

Book Talk

- Ask *What are Jeni and Dad going to do with the new lettuce?* (plant it in the garden) *Will Jeni help Dad plant the new lettuce?* (yes) *When they plant the new lettuce, what do you think will happen?* (The net will protect it.)

- **Phonics Skill** Ask children to find the word *is.* Ask children to find the word *it.* Ask *Which letter is different between those two words?* (the last letter)

Turn to page 14 — Book Talk

"Here is new lettuce for the garden, Jeni," said Dad.

"Dad!" said Jeni. "The birds are looking at the **new** lettuce!"

Revisiting the Text

Future Vocabulary

- Ask children to think about paths. Ask *What does it mean to be on the right path?* (to be doing the correct thing) *Are there right paths and wrong paths?* (Yes, a wrong path might be not eating healthy foods or exercising.)

Now revisit pages 14–15

During Reading

Book Talk

- **Comprehension Strategy** Ask *Can the birds eat the lettuce now?* (no) *Why not?* (Jeni and Dad put a net over the lettuce.)

- **Phonics Skill** Have children locate the word *the*. Ask them to list the new words they can make by adding another letter to the end of this word. *(then, they)*

Turn to page 16 — Book Talk

Jeni and Dad planted the lettuce in the garden.

"This sign can go on the net," said Jeni.

"The birds cannot eat the lettuce now," said Dad.

Revisiting the Text

Future Vocabulary
- Say *Do you think the birds will be unhealthy if they can't eat the lettuce anymore?* (No, they will find other food to eat.)

Go to page T5 – Revisiting the Text

During Reading

Book Talk
- Leave this page for children to discover on their own when they read the book individually.

Individual Reading
Have each child read the entire book at his or her own pace while remaining in the group.

Go to page T5 – Revisiting the Text

 During independent work time, children can read the online book at:
www.rigbyflyingcolors.com

Revisiting the Text

Future Vocabulary
- Use the notes on the right-hand pages to develop oral vocabulary that goes beyond the text. These vocabulary words first appear in future texts. These words are: *morning*, *path*, and *healthy*.

Turn back to page 1

Reading Vocabulary Review
Activity Sheet: Word Web

- Write the word *worked* on the board. Have a volunteer read the word aloud and then use it in a sentence.
- Have children write the word *worked* in the center of the Word Web. Ask children to suggest words to complete the Word Web.

Comprehension Strategy Review
Use Interactive Modeling Card: Venn Diagram

- Demonstrate how to use the Venn Diagram to compare the illustrations on pages 4 and 16 of the book.
- As children compare the two pictures, add their responses to the Venn Diagram.

Phonics Review
- Write the word *ate* on the board. Read the word aloud.
- Ask children to add a letter to the beginning sound to make new words. *(date, mate, rate)*

Fluency Review
- Turn to page 2. Partner children and have them take turns reading the dialogue of Jeni and Dad.
- Remind them how to change voices to differentiate speakers. Then talk about how the different voices make the story more fun to listen to.

Reading-Writing Connection
Activity Sheet: Story Sequence Chart

To assist children with linking reading and writing:
- Use the Story Sequence Chart to discuss the beginning, middle, and end of the story.
- Have children copy phrases from the story onto the chart to complete the story sequence.

4 Assessment

Assessing Future Vocabulary

Work with each child individually. Ask questions that elicit each child's understanding of the Future Vocabulary words. Note each child's responses:

- What school projects have you worked on?
- What is your favorite breakfast food?
- Do you like helping out at home? What sorts of things do you do to help?

Assessing Comprehension Strategy

Work with each child individually. Note each child's understanding of recognizing cause and effect:

- Why did Jeni and Dad need to replant the lettuce?
- Why can't the birds eat the new lettuce?
- Did each child correctly associate causes and effects?

Assessing Phonics

Work with each child individually. Provide each child with magnetic letters. Note each child's responses for understanding adding phonemes to change words:

- Make the word *at* and ask each child to form new words by adding another letter to the beginning of the word.
- Did each child understand that adding only one letter can change the entire word?

Assessing Fluency

Have each child read page 12 to you. Note each child's understanding of changing his or her voice to differentiate speakers:

- Was each child able to vary his or her voice when changing speakers?
- Did each child understand that Dad's voice is lower than Jeni's voice?

Interactive Modeling Cards

Directions: With children, fill in the Word Wheel using the word *healthy*.

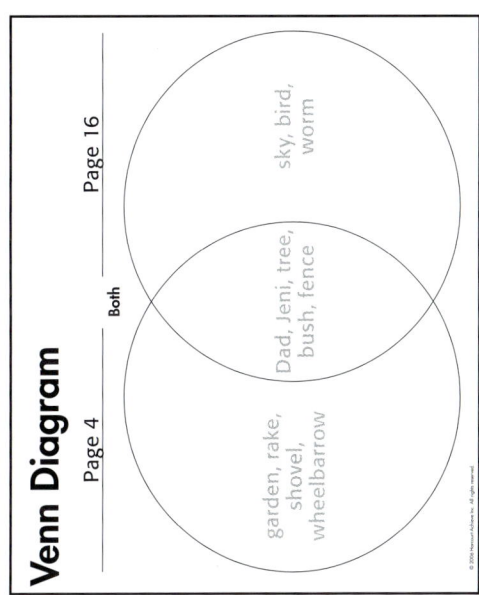

Directions: With children, fill in the Venn Diagram for *Jeni's Lettuce*.

Discussion Questions

- Who were the characters in this book? (Literal)
- What was Jeni's problem in this book? How did she and Dad solve it? (Critical Thinking)
- Do you think Jeni and Dad like to eat lettuce? (Inferential)

T7

Activity Sheets

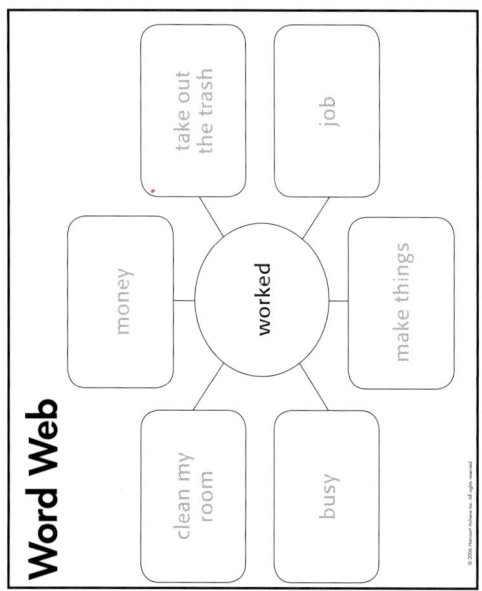

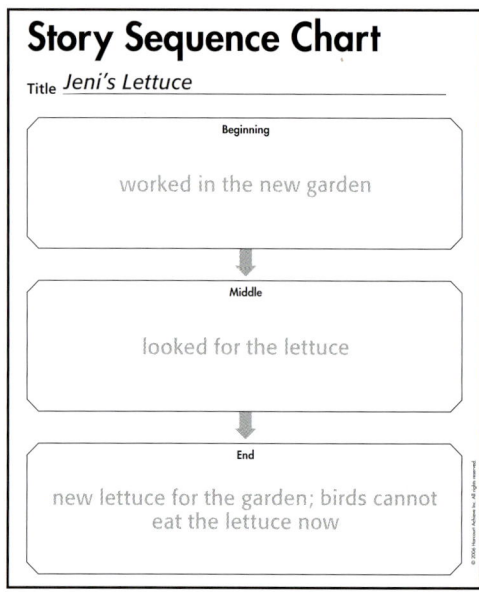

Directions: Have children fill in the Word Web by writing the word *worked* in the center oval, then writing in the rectangles any words or phrases that describe *worked*.

Directions: Have children, independently or with a partner, fill in the Story Sequence Chart by copying phrases from the beginning, middle, and end of the story.
Optional: Have children write an original story using a phrase in the Story Sequence Chart.